the mysterian

BIRDLAND SLIM

FEBRUARY 2002 – APRIL 2005

Contents

1.   WHEN YOU TOOK EVERYTHING

Walk into the sun

My mind is scattered across the world

Like the light of a star

How broken is everything

How perfectly real

And here

And now

Is it all

My mind is made up now

I see you for what you are

And my mind is the one thing

That is still here

When you are gone

-February/2002

2.   THE LAST TIME I SAW YOU THE
SUN WAS IN THE SKY

I can remember the last disciple

The last prayer before the event

Look at the sun

Your eyes shine out of its glow

Where are you now?

When the voodoo comes to greet you

How grandly I will smile

3. I REMEMBER YOU AS A GIRL IN AN ENDLESS
    HALLWAY OF PEOPLE I'VE NEVER SPOKEN TOO

When all I am is a teardrop

When there is nothing between

My eyes and the walls

When the sun rises

And then the moon replaces it

God how useless are my eyes

I have to look through these eyes

Always

My heart

Look at how broken it is

How could anyone repair

My mind sinks into delirium

I talk in conversations

With no one

I am enclosed by these walls

4.   THEY ASKED YOU TO REMEMEBER SOMETHIG
SO BEAUTIFUL THAT YOU ONCE DID, BUT
YOU STARE ONLY BLANKLY AT THE WALL

I link these moments together

By breath

Behind the noise there always

Lays silence

It is our voice that rings

Through the dark hands

That god unfolds around sun and earth

and moon

Look at the stars

How bright they are next to

the immense darkness

There's very little out there

I can remember your face

I remember how soft

And beautiful you were

I try to feel the texture

Of a memory

I try to walk directly

Into the sun

I only want to welcome

A day and a night

Of softness and beauty

No matter how long I live

I will not remember you

i will not remember you

5. YOU CAN WAR OVER THE LAND BUT THERE
    IS ONLY THE EARTH TO RETURN TO

How beautiful and delicate

Is the sky

Look at it there above us

It surrounds completely the sun

It touches all points of the earth

What are you , but the sun

And the earth and the waters

What are you , but everything

That is around you

When did you lose the admission?

Weren't you born here?

Who is more of the earth

Then you ?

When did they take tolerance

From the language?

We could explode like starlight

In a maelstrom of conflict

But, we could only return

to the earth

where we came from

and where we have always only been

6.   6. B.B KING

Through the depths of the blues

Have I travelled

Down to the gin bottle bottom

the sky was not bright

when your music was my aid

It was dark

And no one else was there

Times when only your music

Interlaced my despair

And now I wait patiently

To see you on stage

The actual you

the actual real King of the Blues

In person

I've got a ticket

-May 2002

BIRDLAND SLIM

7.   B.B. KING IN REGINA

I love B.B. King

My eyes as tears

When he plays the blues

Pretty moms in tight dresses

Shaking it to his music

Wow

Beautiful flowers

And the blues Where is all the past?

I only see the shiny future

Wow, I love B.B. King

8.   IN MY DREAM I AM DRUMMING
      FOR THE RAMONES

The Ramones visit me in dreams

I sit round with Joey and Dee Dee

I wake to an empty room

And an outsider in a world

Where there is nothing but inside

I look at your sky

It is the same as my sky

you know how to perform your job

How to communicate

you don't write poetry

I sit here a middle-aged fool

Looking into a broken crystal ball

The world revolves around my feet

Times changes everything here

And in my dreams

I'm drumming for the Ramones

And Dee Dee says "You're our favourite Ramone"

June 4/2002

9. DEE DEE RAMONE HAS DIED

It is a beautiful sunny day

The sky is bright blue

And Dee Dee Ramone has died

From heroin overdose

In Hollywood U.S.A.

How I loved the Ramones

The band from CBGB's

Dee Dee was my all time

Rock 'n Roll hero

I bought a motorcycle jacket

To look like him

I sniffed glue

I spoke to Dee Dee

In dreams

And now he has gone

And a huge empty space

Makes its presence in the world

Somewhere there's an empty

Black leather jacket

And a bass guitar with no sound

I'll look for you Dee Dee

In my punk rock dreams

And on 53rd and 3rd

- June 5/2002

10. END OF THE CENTURY

Somewhere there's two empty

Black leather jackets

And a graffiti lined back alley

Missing its two favourite sons

Don't sniff that glue

Don't go in that pet cemetery

Dee Dee and Joey are gone

let me just sit and play their music

Let me play it and listen to their sound

-June/2002

BIRDLAND SLIM

11. POEM FOR DEE DEE RAMONE

I never once met Dee Dee Ramone

I never once saw the Ramones

On stage

Or in a van

Or even coming out of a Hotel

Or anywhere

I always kept Dee Dee Ramone

In my mind

Now the vampire has sucked

Its toll from your arm

And the needle takes another man

Down in Hollywood, California

My favourite Rock n' Roll hero

They're playing your music

Everywhere

And you are gone

-June/2002

12. "BLACK REBELS MOTORCYCLE CLUB"

The daughter's of the last Czar

Wore pictures of Rasputin

Around their necks

When the Bolsheviks murdered them

Bobby Orr ruined his knees

In the NHL

Long before his time

I stand here a stupid man

How I wish I could be done

With all that

I love

Love

Love

13. 'RIDER PRIDE

Watching from the fourth floor

Parkade Chateau towers

A whino with green hair

And a green 'Rider cap

Asking for booze money

At the liquor board store

He raises his hands overhead

"Touchdown !"

He yells to passing cars

Now there's something you'll only see

In Regina, Sask.

Roughriders win over Calgary

CFL football

14. NIGHT WITH AN ORANGE COLOURED MOON

I am walking home from the ISM building

And the moon is coloured orange

Like a mandarin

I take this oddity of space

As a fortune of good things

To come

-July/2002

Regina

BIRDLAND SLIM

15. THE OLD BELIEVERS

The eve of all that is Great and

beautiful Of all that is lasting

And here

I proclaim I am one

Of the old believers

It is a time of great sorrow

And of sadness

Though tomorrow the sun

Will rise

And there will be great

Things

BIRDLAND SLIM

16. WE HAVE A STRONG LOVE

We have a strong love

Unbroken by time or distance

Unbroken by failure

Unbroken by mistakes

Unbroken by the odds

Unbroken by the modern world

Unbroken by anything

We have a strong love

My family is connected

By only love

We have a strong love

A love that exists

Exists nowhere else

On this blue and only earth

BIRDLAND SLIM

17.   OUR LOVE

Our love

Is a field where there

Is only sunshine

And flowers

And two people kissing

And smooching and embracing

That is our love

-August/2002

34

18. IF YOU HAD OUR LOVE YOU WOULD
     BE HAPPY ALL THE TIME

If you had our love

You'd never be sad

If you had our love

Your world would be

Sunshine and roses

And white clouds in a blue sky

That's what it would

Be like

If you had our love

But, you don't

You don't

Have

Our

Love

19.   MY DAUGHTER IS FIVE YEARS OLD

Your love is the sunshine

And the blue sky

And earth, where, look...

There you are !

Its your birthday

Only on this world do you live

And all good things gravitate

Towards you

How beautiful is everything

With you in this world

How light is Time when you are near

How long the distance between

Where you stand and my eyes

And how strong the love is

That touches us and knows

No distance that is not overcome

-August 18/2002

20.   POEM FOR GEK SPARROW

We smoked marijuana together

In my dream

And you were sitting at a table

And everything was fine

And I was with my daughter

In your kitchen

That was in my dream

And thank-you for visiting me

There, my friend

-August 21/2002

Regina

I'm at the Saskatchewan Roughrider football game against the Montreal Alouettes. Some cute girls are walking by on the field holding a large sign. The loud speakers Are playing "Blitzkrieg Bop" by the Ramones. Wow. I'm sitting in the cheap seats

In the end zone. The benches are coloured orange and the paint is peeling off. Taylor Field, Regina Sask.

August/2002

I'm watching the traffic on Broad street from the fourth

level of the parkade

Of the Chateau Tower office building above Bartleby's

nightclub. Down the street I see three bikers coming on

big Harley-Davidsons. When they pass by I see on the

Backs of their vests "Hells Angels –Regina" August/2002

BIRDLAND SLIM

21. TOGETHER

And there's my little girl

She's as sweet as a flower

In the spring

Where her smile is

There are my eyes

there is no sadness in the world

When we are together

there are no tears

In anyone's eyes

When we are together

The sun is in the sky

BIRDLAND SLIM

22. FOREVER CONSTANTLY THE WORLD IS AT WAR

Forgotten countries

Human lives starving

In desert and jungle

And we are here

With our planned obsolescence

And waste that spreads around everything

The world goes around in a circle

There is nowhere else to live

They are just over there

The starving people

We have sixteen thousand boxes

Of everything

Our garbage dumps reach to the sky

46

23. THOSE WHO RUN BETWEEN DREAMS
SEEKS THOSE WHO LONG FOR SLEEP

You cannot hide from those

Who run between dreams

It is my finger pointing at you

Look at how you are covered by sun

Where can you go to

Now that I have found

The distance to your dream

You will never understand sleep again

Or call your memories to your self

What you are is a measure of sunlight

In a deep sky

You will see my eyes in your dream

They will be as the sun and moon

They will be as the earth and sea

24. FOR MY FATHER

My Father's life has gone

He is now of the sky

He is now of the sun

The waters and the earth

He is of memory and dream

He is of beauty and silence

And eternity

My father is the sunlight

And the clouds

My Father's life has gone

-January 20/2003

BIRDLAND SLIM

25. POEM FOR JOE STRUMMER

Joe Strummer has died

And somewhere there is sky

Without clouds

Teenagers sitting in a basement

Smoking pot and listening to

The Clash

Somewhere the poor are hungry

Somewhere the clampdown weighs down

Round and round there is the sound

Of "London Calling"

Somewhere there is sunshine

Without clouds

And Joe Strummer has died

Joe Strummer has died

52

26. THEY SAID THE WHOLE WORLD
IS GOING TO EXPLODE

AND I SAID "OKAY"

My mind is silicone

A wandering Jew in a series

Of hallways

Look at all the beautiful things

They put just out of reach

The sun is so far away

How can anyone exist here

You are a composite

Of what they've sold you

You are the end result of their imagination

You are nothing but the truth and a lie

BIRDLAND SLIM

27. THEY WILL PLACE YOU WHERE THEY
     FEEL YOU ARE NECESARY

They put their white-out over me

They said I got into the wrong line

I had not achieved their criteria

They closed the door

I turned around

And saw a street made in their progress

This is where my new life lay

Thie is where I was supposed to live

BIRDLAND SLIM

28. PULLING DOWN STATUES

They are pulling down

The statue of Saddam Hussein

In Baghdad today

The leader is under his pile of rubble

Where has he gone?

Where to now?

Are we not all alone here

Are we not all together here

This is the waging of war

There are people dancing

In the streets over there

There are people watching

Their T.V. sets

Over here

-April/2003

BIRDLAND SLIM

29. SELLING MY HOUSE

In my home

Home become a house

Behind are left scarred memories

Left on dark hangers

In now deserted closets

Close the doors

Throw away the keys

Put the "for sale" sign

On the front lawn

I came to reclaim what

Was once mine

And now I'm letting go

Now I'm letting go

-June 7/2003

OTTAWA STREET, REGINA

30. LOOKING AT THIS HOUSE WHICH
     WAS ONCE A HOME TO ME

An older, wiser, dumber man

I can look and see

It's time to run away and flee

This house is no home to me

There are memories and memories

That cover every wall

But, I look around here

And all I see is an empty house

And me

Look out the window

See the tired prostitutes

Worry themselves down the avenue

Look at the pimp in his red bandana

Rides past on a bicycle

Cold eyes stare and die

Across the neighbourhood

He surveys the landscape

Look at the children

Across the alley

Playing in the broken furniture

Syringes lying by the garbage

goodbye

This house is for sale

I can't live here anymore

-June 7/2003

31. HOUSE

This house is the end of my

Eyes

It is the feeling at the end

of my touch

This house is where I am

Living now

My beautiful house

This house is my memory

I breathe and I breathe

In this house

-June/2003

BIRDLAND SLIM

32. STILL HERE STILL

To forget yesterday

To rip the sun from the sky

To remember nothing

To never admit your presence

Before my eyes again

To live forever beneath

Sun and moon and sky

I could throw away Time

Live only in dream and memory

My life supported by your kisses

And touch

But, truly

Here I am

BIRDLAND SLIM

33. ON FINDING NEEDLES BY MY
     HOUSE ON CANADA DAY

Five, six needles

Scattered around two vials

Of T&R's

Right in the side alley

Between my house and the next

Bloody kleenex

they were shooting up here

Today is Canada day

I'm standing here looking

At this shit

I call the Fire dept.

To take away the junk

The firefighters are even surprised

To see this sadness

Junk is no good

Junk is wrong

-July 1/2003

Ottawa street, Regina

34. BAD NEIGHBOURS

A broken man

Rebuilding his life fragment by fragment

Piece by piece

Brick by solid brick

I can see the sun rising

The rock bottom appearing

Smaller and smaller below my feet

Look at all the new things I have now

Look at all the ghosts

That crowd the storage rooms

Of my past

Ha ! They're just ghosts

Fading in the hallways of my memory

I'm here

They left nothing but their

Ghosts

35. AMORPHON

It was ten years ago

Today

That Dadeo-4-Cube

Performed Amorphon

At the Bridge gallery

11th avenue

Hot night

Mosquitos like rain

The little gallery

Cut-out pictures adorning

All the walls

Two-hundred people crammed

Into that little gallery

-July/2003

72

73

PART TWO:

"EASTVIEW"

BIRDLAND SLIM

36. WINTER BABY

I was born in the winter

In the cold and the dark

My Mother 30 hours in labour

I am not of the summer

I do not know the sun

I know the snow

And the cold

I know the dark moon

And the empty street

76

37. ALL AROUND THEY PUT THINGS ONE
     CANNOT REACH OR TOUCH

here are only so many things

There are only so many skies

The sun there it is

Right above you

That's what is keeping you alive

How real are your dreams

And your memories

I can remember being with a young woman

She was so beautiful

But, then where is she now?

To end all the memories

To say goodbye to it all

To start somewhere new

How lucky I am

How alive and well I feel

-September/2003

Broder Street, Regina

38. HOME

Here I am in my new home

Here everything is mine

Here everything is here

And around me and real

Look, here is my heart

I can put my things just

where they should go

I can do my laundry here

This is my home

October/2003

Broder street

BIRDLAND SLIM

39. FIVE HOUSES DOWN

I am standing outside my home

I'm drinking a beer

With my neighbour

A Hell's Angel

Drives down the street

On a red Harley-Davidson

He lives five houses down

From me

Dark night and lights

BIRDLAND SLIM

40. I LOVE MY NEW HOME

I love my new home

And every room and thing in it

I love my neighbourhood

And the Hell's Angel

Down the street

I love the trains that rumble

Past my house

I love the dogs that bark

I love the scrapyards

I love the metal works

I love everything that is here

I love my new home

-October/2003

Broder street

BIRDLAND SLIM

41. DRIVING DOWN BRODER

Early morning

Grey cloudy skies

Drive past the trains

American cattle transport cars

Rusty metal Regina Motorcycle Salvage

Beautiful day

Beautiful day

-October 25/2003

42. FIRST SNOWFALL BRODER STREET

The snowflakes fall and cover

My car

I go out to the backyard

Railcars in the distance

White iron

The sky black and long

Points of stars

Whisps of clouds

i love it here

This is where i am now

This is where I am now

BIRDLAND SLIM

43. LISTENING TO THE RADIO

I'm in my new home

And the Regina Pats

Are on the radio

I have the lights on in the kitchen

And my neighbours are outside drinking

The Pats score a goal

And the other team scores a goal

The Saskatchewan Roughriders didn't

Make it to the Grey Cup

But, that's the same as every year

Its Grey Cup week in Regina

I heard this all on the radio

My little radio

In the kitchen of my new home

My neighbours are outside

Drinking beer

BIRDLAND SLIM

Its cool and snow is on the ground

There are railcars near my home

And the Regina Pats are on the radio

And I'm listening in the kitchen

Of my new home

-November 10/2003

44. POEM FOR RHONDA

I still see you in dreams

Time is mounting between us

There's nothing left of you

in my world, except dreams

Wow, what a beautiful, wonderful

Person you were

I'm alone here

If we could return to our

Summer of love I would

You're just a ghost

What am I some kind of

Fool still dreaming of you

That was so long ago

I have to live my life without you

Who wrote the story that it

Should be so

I'm middle aged and so are

You

You don't remember me

And I'm here writing a poem

For you

-November/2003

BIRDLAND SLIM

45. FOR MY FRIEND DARCY WHO WROTE
     ME A LETTER SAYING HE IS DYING

Only in my dreams now

Am I being robbed

My new house is Home

Refuge, sanctuary, outline

Of my existence, soul, heart

You are a long ways away

In Victoria

You say you are dying

This can't be so

Don't leave me here alone

On this world

Who am I to tell my troubles to

In my mind

You're my best friend

-November/2003

Regina

46. NOTHING SEPERATES US AND THIS
     IS WHAT I DON'T UNDERSTAND

Here is my little world

All the sky is beautiful here

Isn't everything wonderful

Isn't everything great

I see that there is a moon

Above me

And earth below my feet

You are there I want to touch you

You are just there and beautiful

There is a separation of space

Between us

There are too many people here

Give me an empty world

Where there is only you

And me

BIRDLAND SLIM

47. TO BE IN ONE'S OWN HOME IS TO
     LOOK AT THE WALLS AND

     THE FLOORS AND SMILE

     AND LAUGH AND CRY

     We are the measurement of Time

     The distance between here and

     Where you are is Time

     Here I am in heaven sitting down

     Standing on the wood floors

     Of my own home

     I have me piece of dry land

     The hard waters levelling

     Away from me

     I could stay here forever

     You won't come here

     And for this I say "Thank you"

48. NOVEMBER ROAD TRIP – REGINA PATS

Pats on the radio

Season 2003/2004

Long road trip

B.C. teams this year

Radio only brings in

Bad news

Loss after loss

Josh Harding can't stop all

The pucks

-November/2003

49. FOR THE BEAUTIFUL WOMEN
OF THE AGRIDOME

The beautiful women of the Agridome

Walk past two on beautiful two

I'm standing against the rail

There's a woman in a yellow t-shirt

As beautiful as a summer sun

But, now it is winter time

And she goes and sits across

On the other side of the arena

The Pats battle the Vancouver Giants

And MVP goalie Josh Harding has gone

To the baby Nats training camp

The Pats lose 6-3

On teddy bear toss night

The beautiful woman

In the yellow t-shirt sits way on the other side

Of the arena

And the beautiful women of the Agridome

Leave the arena two on beautiful

Two

-December/2003

Agridome

50. VOW TO THE MUSE OF POETRY

Long ago

I took a vow

To remain faithful to

The muse of poetry

A tall Greek statue

In a Toronto museum

But the muse herself

Is a jealous lover

And she will not share you

With another

To a beautiful poem sweetly

Does she come

And my love affair with her

I pray is never done

51. ONCE I WAS THROWN INTO THE GUTTER

Once I was thrown head long

Onto a black Corvette

And into the gutter

Outside the Jolly Roger bar

That was a long time ago

And now my Eastview home enwraps

Itself around me

Like a warm embrace

This is my love

This is my home

Where can I go where I can

See something more welcome

Then this

These walls, these floors, these ceiling

52.   WRITTEN ON THE DAY THEY
      TRADED JOSH HARDING

The goal net is empty at the Agridome

Josh Harding has been traded to the Wheat kings

I saw Ed Staniowski play goal

And I saw Bart Hunter play goal

And I saw Josh Harding play goal

And the net is empty now at the Agridome

Josh first made a name on the

U.S. road trip of 2003/2004

The Pats set a team record for the most

Wins on the road

His star rose from then on

Drafted by the Minnesota wild

Most career shutouts for a Pat

Junior World's in Helsinki

there I was standing by the rail

At the Agridome watching the warm-up

There you were standing in goal

You stopped shot after shot

I stood with all the others

In the crowd watching you

Play goal

For the Regina Pats

-January 7/2004

53. NEW ERA- PATS VS KAMLOOPS BLAZERS

The trades have been made

The players have left the players

Have arrived

Dustin Slade is the new goalie

Still wearing his Kamloops Blazer

Goalie mask and equipment

I watch the warm-up from the rails

He looks good

I'm impressed

There's Kamloops –a strong team

From a strong B.C. division

You've got to move on

You've got to keep going

To the next day

Pats win

BIRDLAND SLIM

54. SUN SETTING SUN RISING

I feel like the sun

I feel like the morning

This is a new day

And i have arrived here

Waiting to collect all the beautiful things

That have been kept from me

For so long

No one understands how much solitude

It takes to write a poem

How many drunken nights

Alone beneath a silvery moon

Here are my poems for you

They are all love poems

I wrote them for you

-January/2004

BIRDLAND SLIM

55. ISHI HAS DIED

I can remember seeing the sun

And blue skies and clouds

I remember seeing a beautiful woman

Her eyes like two beautiful moons

Seeing her was like drinking tea

In a forest filled with snow

Wow

I remember an empty room

I remember people who never spoke I

remember streets and buildings

And T.V. sets that were never

Turned off

I stand in a river of sadness

And all that there is to see

Are two eyes

Filled with tears

and i know they are yours

56. COLD, COLD DAY JOSH HARDING
     RETURNS TO THE DOME

I'm outside the Agridome

Warming my car between periods

-36c

Josh Harding's return to Regina

Now with the Brandon Wheat kings

The sky is low and cold

Smoke billows from the orange

Agridome roof

People smoke outside the doors

In the cold

This is beautiful

-January 28/2004

BIRDLAND SLIM

57. KISSING THE BOTTLE GOODBYE

A prairie wind levels my thoughts and mind

Sobriety a vacuum

The monkey is getting anxious

There's nothing but dry desert

Dry sky

Outside my house the snow is melting

A new spring

How beautiful it is not to drink

To live and breathe

Everything seems empty

Everything seems a new start

A new page

A new day without booze

-May/2004

BIRDLAND SLIM

58. MOOSE JAW WARRIORS SWEEP
THE REGINA PATS 4-0

The Agridome is finished

The Moose Jaw Warriors sweep

the Pats

Right off the ice

Moose Jaw fans clap

And cheer and wave their

Little banners in the air

And I'm sitting here

Wearing my Pats jersey

This is my home arena

This is the bottom

-March 24/2004

Agridome Regina

59. SOMETIMES

Sometimes I still imagine us

Making love

Sometimes I still think of you

In my mind

Sometimes I wonder where you are

Here I am approaching 40

My time with you was long ago

But, it seems as though it was yesterday

Wow how beautiful you were

I can still how soft you were

In my touch

What do you mean to me now

A ghost an image

An empty space

A lost moment never recovered

A day when there was sunlight

Soft rain under summer moonlight

-April/2004

60. A NIGHT OF BOOZE AFTER NOT
     DRINKING FOR 2 ½ WEEKS

The flame that ignites my mind

Seems so familiar and friendly

And warm

Here I am drunk again

Here I am alone again

Its just one night

I progress forward

Where will I be in one year

Where will I be in two

I stack up more and more days

With no booze

Tonight I am drunk

But, I made this choice

But, until next payday

I won't have another

Slowly, slowly I win this game

The monkey will leave me for another

Slowly, slowly I shake this booze

-April/2004

61. ON SEEING A MAN JUMP FROM A
     BUILDING ON EASTER SUNDAY

Today I saw a man jump to his death

From a downtown Hotel

His dead body still and lifeless in the parking

Lot

The police sirens and ambulance

The yellow tape

Street gawkers

They placed a white sheet over his body

And left him there on the dark pavement

Easter, Sunday

Regina, Sask.

-April 11/2004

62.   SUICIDE HOTEL

Fall fall

From the suicide Hotel

Break break

Your heart

The sun shines

The world divides (collides)

And there is nothing but darkness

There are people who are left behind

Don't take that leap

Don't suffer that fall

There's sadness for those left behind

There's nothing in it for you

Suicide is against you

Only life will give you anything

Only by staying alive can you win

When you are alive

You can do something

You can change something

63. "BIG DIG SEQUENCE"

1. BEGINNING OF THE BIG DIG

Early morning darkness 5:30 A.M.

Going to the building where I work

Pass by Wascana creek

Spotlights of the big dig

I see the lights of the big machines

By the creek

-Wascana, Broad street bridge

Regina

2. WINTER DIG

Each morning I pass the cold darkness

The dig at Wascana creek

The cold lights the endless cycle

Of trucks

They're getting further from the bridge

During the day old men line the creek

Watching the big machines

-December/2003

3. EVEN IN THE COLD, COLD THEY STAND

    AND WATCH THE DIG

Cold winds blow in the winter

Drive by the Broad street bridge

Cars and cars line the bridge

People standing in the winter cold

Watching the heavy machinery

Move tonne after tonne of rich soil

Its cold, cold outside

4. LOOKING OUT OVER THE BIG DIG

Looking out from the observation point

Where I once kissed with Rhonda

On a sunny summer evening

Now it is winter and Wascana

Is empty of water

Little dumptrucks and bulldozers

Roll along slowly over the dark earth

The big dig in full steam

How impressive it is

-APRIL/2004

64. ON SEEING THE REGINA SILVER
     FOXES PLAY HOCKEY

I'm sitting with my Father at the Al Ritchie arena

In the mid 1970's

The Regina Silver Foxes are skating

Around the ice during warm-up

The have green uniforms with silver trim

The goalie has a gold coloured mask

In my memory the opposition wears

Red Detroit Red Wings uniforms

The Weyburn Red Wings?

The Silver Foxes are in the middle

Of setting a record for consecutive losses

It was in the newspaper

And I remember telling my Dad about it

My Dad didn't like Hockey

He liked Football

But, he took me to see the Silver Foxes

That was the only time he took me to

A Hockey game

The Silver Foxes lost

I was a witness

65. I AM ALONE AND YOU ARE
     SOMEWHERE ELSE ALONE

In the Joy Division of my mind

Four walls oppose every movement

How the sky is so endless

Rituals so enduring

the music is a nail driven in wood

The music is the falling to sleep

As the night is dark and forever starlight

Pages torn away

In the Joy Division of my mind

Four walls separate me

Your pretty eyes somewhere

The air and the clouds in the sky

Are the distance

Between our hearts

BIRDLAND SLIM

66. ON MEETING CLARK GILLIES AND GETTING
     HIS AUTOGRAPH ON A HOCKEY STICK

After weeks of rain

It was a bright July day

In Moose Jaw, Sask.

It was "Clark Gillies day"

They named the park with the baseball diamond

And the outdoor rink "Clark Gillies rec. Area"

I'm standing there waiting with my stick

1974 Regina Pats Memorial Cup champs

Clark was one of five who hadn't signed it

So, I'd gone to Moose Jaw to get his autograph

What a big man

Four Stanley cup rings

He donated one million dollars

To start a children's hospital in New York

Here he was a normal guy and talking to everyone

Shaking hands

I showed him my old Hockey stick

And he signed it like it was no big deal

He shook my hand

-July 9/2004

Best Wishes
Lloyd
Gilmour
COMPLIMENTS OF COLGATE

67. FOR TAMRA KEEPNESS

Where are you little girl?

People are looking through all the streets for you

You just vanished

You lived just down the street

From my old home

And now you are gone

And no one knows were you are

Where have you gone?

In my dreams I take you up

The stairs of your home

Your Mother is there so happy to see you

But, In this dark world

I don't know where you are

And I feel like nothing

I feel like I can't do anything

-July 12/2004

68. A STONE FOR JOHNNY RAMONE

Bowery CBGB's

the man with the cardboard guitar

Buzzsaw architecture

Electric chainsaw

The heart of the Ramones

the man who directed the van

Down the long rock n' roll highway

You've passed away now

Leaving us all alone

The Mosrite is silent now

The Ramones are gone

Forever there won't be anyone like you

I blew my ears out listening to your music

I had every album

R.I.P. Johnny Ramone

- September 15/2004

Johnny Ramone died in L.A. Of cancer

Kenneth Patchen
Selected Poems

69. NEW SEASON PATS LOSE – SEPT./2004

Walking to the Agridome

Pass the old buildings on the exhibition grounds

Warm autumn weather wearing no coat

Looking for familiar faces in the crowd

The Pats are very young this year

Many new faces

This team should be good a couple of seasons

From now

I'm watching Logan Pyett in the warm-up

Last season I watched him with the Midgett AAA

Pat Canadians

I told my son about him

This team should be good a couple

of seasons from now

They are all just a bunch of kids

The Pats lose to the Wheat KIngs 4-2

After the game I buy some beer

At the Empire off-sale

The Cree woman at the checkout

Is very beautiful

70. EASTVIEW-ONE YEAR

The Hell's Angel has a new motorcycle

The cat who lives under the house

Is sleeping on my sofa

The leaves are covering the weeds

On the front lawn

How beautiful are the women I see everywhere

Life is endless

Nothing will ever change

The sun is in the sky

How I long for things that are not here

Just to hold them in my arms

This world is sick and dark

My mind is slowly forgetting

Its direction

I have lived here for one year now

And I am very happy to be here

-September 30/2004

Broder street

71. STRANGE LITTLE GIRL

My eyes embedded in a broken heart

My time released in a thunderstorm of nothing

Blue sanctuary

I have nothing to say to anyone

Anymore

Your voice is a sound I hide from

Leave me alone

I don't want to understand

Your understanding

Your world has nothing to do

With me

Who are you to judge

I don't judge you

72. ON SEEING THE EVERETT SILVERTIPS
    FIRST GAME AT THE AGRIDOME

Walking past the old buildings

Of Exhibition park

The crumbling decaying bricks

How long have these buildings been here?

This is Saskatchewan

Things are old here

Not everything is new here

The sky is dark

November Hockey

The Pats warm-up in the traditional blues

At the far end are the Everett Silvertips

The WHL's newest team

I look at the banners overhead

And the beautiful women who come

the Agridome

There are a lot of scouts here tonight

The Pats lose 5-1 in an unexciting game

-November 12/2004

73. ROUGHRIDERS-25 B.C. LIONS-27

My heart is broken

And it is cold outside

And the 'Riders have lost

Its not fair

The B.C. lions are the scourge of the

West

Its going to be a long winter

And the future is uncertain

November 14/2004

Western final, CFL

158

74. TSUNAMI DEC. 26/2004

On the otherside of the world

People drown in a snowstorm of sea

Whole villages just wiped away

So many orphans and lost souls

The childless parents

Caring for the orphaned children

As their own

BIRDLAND SLIM

75. FOR RHONDA

I wake each morning thinking of you

You are gone from me

I can hardly remember you accurately anymore

You are part of me like

The cold t-shirt I put on each morning

I go to work each day

I don't come home to you

So what?

Where are you?

You are not here

And what can I do about it

-January/2005

BIRDLAND SLIM

76. ON SEEING "END OF THE CENTURY"
    AT THE REGINA PUBLIC LIBRARY

I am sitting down in a seat

At the Regina Public Library

I've come here to watch

A film about the Ramones

"End of the Century"

I look around the theatre

The audience is mostly men

Men sitting alone like myself

The Ramones were my favourite band

I've had their records for 25 years

Now here I am in this library theatre

To watch a documentary about them

Three of them are dead now

Johnny, Joey and Dee Dee

They're gone now

The lights go down and the film

Begins

When it's over I go home

Feeling proud

And beautiful

-January 20/2005

77. ON LEARNING OF THE DEATH OF B.B. GABOR

Flipping through the internet

B.B. Gabor webpage

The Toronto police found him dead

In his apartment suicide 1990

What happened to B.B. Gabor?

Nyet Nyet Soviet

I played his record again and again

New Wave Toronto punk

Moscow Drug Club

Balalaika New Wave

I can't believe B.B. Gabor is dead

So long I had wondered what

had happened to him

Suicide in his Toronto apartment
I can't believe how sad that is

-February/2005

BIRDLAND SLIM

78. ON LOOSING HENRY BURRIS TO
THE CALGARY STAMPEDERS

Seeing Henry Burris in a black Stetson

Red Stampeder uniform

now that's sad

That isn't what anyone wanted to see

Coming so close in the "04 Grey cup semi-final

Now going over to the vampire

That lives in Saskatchewan blood

Calgary

Its always this way in the Rider nation

They break our hearts

Life isn't fair

-February 25/2005

BIRDLAND SLIM

79. ON SEEING MY HELL'S ANGELSS
    NEIGHBOUR AND HIS DAUGHTER

I'm working downtown on the weekend

I see at the Hotel across the backalley

The Hell's Angels are inducting 4 new members

I see the Hell's Angel who lives

On the next block from me

He's there with his three year old daughter

They walk together into the Hotel

He's wearing a Hell's Angels t-shirt

There must be 30 or 40 Hell's Angels there

-March 5/2005

80. X- FOR EXENE CERVENKA

X ruled the planet like cats amongst

Mice

And the radio is silent of them

Why?

Why Madonna?

And not Exene?

Die, die radio die

Radio is plastic and hollow and sad

X is not heard there

Their music was everything

That classic rock never was

If I hear AC/DC one more time

I think I'll throw up

-April/2005

81. IF IT WASN'T FOR THIS MOON
     AND THESE STARS

I remember being young and pissing

In a stall in the bathroom of a bar

Looking at myself in the bathroom mirror

and thinking what a good looking guy

Wow! Life is the only thing we know

There's beautiful women everywhere

Breathe in that air

There's lips everywhere to kiss

Life is everything

What else do we know of

What else can we do

Where else can we live

But here

BIRDLAND SLIM is one of the world's few

remaining Genuine poets. He did not study

poetry he lived poetry.He has known unrequited

love and held his broken heart In his hand. He

did not study the poets he lived with them.

He does not like poetry or poets.

He is tired of their weakness

And their shallowness. He wants to see

a poets heart there before him

In their poems but sadly, he is always

left wanting. Poetry to him

Is seeing a woman on a bus with eyes

like two moons and knowing

You will never see her again.